# Southeast Asian Studies:
# Reorientations

**Frank H. Golay, 1915-1990**

# SOUTHEAST ASIAN STUDIES: REORIENTATIONS

CRAIG J. REYNOLDS
RUTH MCVEY

THE FRANK H. GOLAY
MEMORIAL LECTURES
2 AND 3

SOUTHEAST ASIA PROGRAM PUBLICATIONS
Southeast Asia Program
Cornell University
Ithaca, New York

Editorial Board
    Benedict Anderson
    George Kahin
    Stanley O'Connor
    Keith Taylor
    Oliver Wolters

Cornell Southeast Asia Program Publications
640 Stewart Avenue, Ithaca, NY 14850-3857

Frank H. Golay Memorial Lectures 2 and 3

The Frank H. Golay Memorial Lecture Series
has been made possible through
a generous donation from
the Frank H. Golay Memorial Endowment.

© 1998 Cornell Southeast Asia Program.

All rights reserved. Except for brief quotations in a review, no part of this book may be reproduced or utilized in any form or by any means, electronic or mechanical, including photocopying and recording, or by any information storage or retrieval system, without permission in writing from the Cornell Southeast Asia Program.

ISBN 0-87727-301-4

Cover Design: Ragiidup (Tobabatak). Pattern of a traditional cloth to help maintain a firm spirit.

# Contents

Self-Cultivation and Self-Determination
in Postcolonial Southeast Asia     7
*Craig J. Reynolds*

Globalization, Marginalization, and
the Study of Southeast Asia     37
*Ruth McVey*

Frank H. Golay Biography and Bibliography     65

# SELF-CULTIVATION AND SELF-DETERMINATION IN POSTCOLONIAL SOUTHEAST ASIA

## Craig J. Reynolds[1]

The organizers of the annual Golay Memorial Lecture have a long list of potential speakers to choose from, so I feel very honored to have been invited to give the second lecture. I grew up in this part of the world, and I always like to come back, though I have to say the sweet nostalgia is mixed with the memory of dreading some returns to Ithaca. My teachers are now friends and colleagues, but I can still recall rushing to complete late term papers and cramming for what used to be called the "A" exam. I think it was Jane Austen who said that one

---

[1] In revising the lecture for publication I have benefited from the comments of a number of colleagues who patiently read earlier drafts or suggested references and perspectives: Virginia Hooker, Ward Keeler, Tom Kirsch, Ruth McVey, Leslie Morris, O. W. Wolters.

does not love a place the less for having suffered in it, and so it is with my feelings for Ithaca.

Professor Thorbecke, who gave the inaugural Golay Memorial Lecture and spoke about "The Political Economy of Development," sensibly confined himself to the comparison of two countries, Indonesia and the Philippines. Venturing to the edges of my expertise in the spirit of the education I received when I was a student in the Southeast Asia Program, I have decided to use this opportunity to speak comparatively about the region in the twentieth century.

I have fretted about the cumbersome and verbose title, because "self" is a woolly concept. While it has been deconstructed to death and its analytic powers challenged, "self" has reemerged in the current fashion for identity politics and the debates about Asian values.[2] One might think that "self-determination" is something *most* Southeast Asians staked out for themselves long ago, but the recent history of East Timor, the Karen and Dayak peoples, and even the nation-state of Cambodia should give us pause before we declare the end of self-determination as a motive force in the region. "Self-cultivation" is suspect as an analytical tool for studying Southeast Asian mentalities and movements, being seen

---

[2] The anthropologist Melford Spiro has been highly critical of the simplistic dichotomy of Western and non-Western self, calling it "wildly overdrawn." In this dichotomy the Western self tends to be characterized as individuated, differentiated, and autonomous, whereas the non-Western self is interdependent and exhibits a fluid self-other boundary. Spiro argues that the differences within these sets are as great as the differences across them. See his "Is the Western Conception of the Self 'Peculiar' within the Context of World Culture?" *Ethos*, 21 (1993): 107–53. The problematic of self-making as a rhetorical practice is framed in a recent volume of essays edited by Debbora Battaglia, *Rhetorics of Self-Making* (Berkeley: University of California Press, 1995).

as something Californians do with crystals, hashish, and their personal aerobics instructors. But I hope to show in the following discussion the connection between self-cultivation and Southeast Asia's self-determination in the postcolonial epoch.

My aim is to sketch a history in Southeast Asia for the cluster of values and practices represented by such terms as self-cultivation, self-determination, self-assurance, self-reliance, self-strengthening, self-discipline, self-denial, self-improvement, and self-development at the individual, community, and national level. Living in Australia, where there has been since the mid-1980s an ongoing, bipartisan debate about the country's "engagement with Asia," I am particularly conscious of postcolonial assertiveness on the part of Southeast Asian leaders. In highly publicized incidents public officials in Indonesia, Malaysia, and Thailand have challenged Australian comprehension of the culture and institutions of their respective countries. Behind the rhetoric about "Asian values," a rhetoric that may be hypocritically invoked to mask brutalities and injustice, lie genuine cultural differences, linguistic barriers, and local practices that challenge the best ethnography to interpret them.

As I shall explain in a minute, the topic of this lecture called to me from one of Frank Golay's books, but to prepare me to hear this call were two articles in the popular press. One was a piece in *The Economist*, which began as follows:

> The countries of South-East Asia have rarely controlled their own destinies. Asia's three giants—China, Japan and India—loom over the region. Colonial armies have fought there. Even peace and unprecedented prosperity have not shaken the

assumption that South-East Asia's fate will be decided by outsiders.³

The countries of Southeast Asia have rarely controlled their own destinies? Southeast Asia's fate will be decided by outsiders? I do not see parts of Southeast Asia any more or less enmeshed in—or determined by—global economic forces, telecommunications technology, and so forth than other parts of the world. To be sure, most of Southeast Asia was colonized by the Western imperial powers—directly, partially, or indirectly—and is now largely decolonized. At various times there have been pockets of compromised sovereignty (foreign bases, for example), and neocolonialism in various forms is still an issue for Southeast Asian governments. Multi-national enterprises, debates over human rights, and even regional economic cooperation have been targets of the charge that the West is interfering in domestic politics. But the claims by *The Economist*'s journalist that Southeast Asian countries have not controlled their own destiny seemed extreme.

Then, in an article in the *Canberra Times*, I read a remarkable headline: "Cambodia looks at becoming a giant theme park":

> The Cambodian Government is considering an enormously expensive, radical proposal from a conservation organization to turn the entire country into a giant theme park based on nature and ancient Khmer culture. The unprecedented idea for the "World National Park" suggests that Cambodia adopt an "alternative development plan" and forget about developing industrially, according to a preliminary proposal from the Society for Ecology

---

³ *The Economist*, June 24, 1995, p. 16.

and Wildlife Preservation in Cambodia. Instead, it should put all its energy into protecting its environment and history, the plan says.

"This is not a 'pie in the sky' proposal," the director of the society, Marshall Perry, said. "But for it to work, the Government has to be fully committed to it—the whole ball of wax." What some might consider handicaps for any other country—lack of development and infrastructure—were actually advantages for the plan to work in Cambodia, he said.[4]

The proposal called for the international community to pay for the estimated five billion dollars it will cost over a five-year transition period during which industry would be marginalized, then eliminated. Cambodian opinion on the proposal, such as it was reported in the newspaper article, was mixed. One Cambodian official welcomed it as "a good idea," while another dismissed it, saying, "I don't think it will fly."

The idea of turning a sovereign nation into a giant theme park may be well-intentioned in its vision to save Cambodia from the ills of modern development. But the assumption that the "international community" can control the fate of a country is alarming. One can imagine the theme park being sold off to an international consortium of park developers. Australian investors enticed to the project would stock the barays with fresh water crocodiles, and emus would roam through the temple ruins. So, in view of this particular plan to deal with Cambodia's present problems, perhaps the statement in *The Economist* that Southeast Asia's fate will be decided by outsiders is not so extreme after all.

---

[4] *The Canberra Times*, August 7, 1995.

Old colonial conceits linger in the fantasies of developers and theme park managers.

In any case, I was struck by how resilient the theme of self-determination is with respect to Southeast Asia. It appears in a book Frank Golay co-edited, where he talks of the "smallness" of Southeast Asian states, with the exception of Vietnam and possibly Indonesia. Golay does not see this "smallness" in terms of area or population. Instead, he says, these states "must be assessed as 'small' in terms of dimensions of strength which can be mobilized to ensure their continued existence as independent states."[5] The implication of Golay's remark is that self-determination for most Southeast Asian countries was constrained by their "strength" relative to other countries in Asia and the rest of the world.

**Area Studies and Theory**

Frank Golay's comment about relative strength hints at the issue of security and sovereignty, the issue, if you will, of the vulnerability of Southeast Asian countries. The vulnerability of Southeast Asia is also at stake in present debates about knowledge of the region, what we commonly refer to as area studies. In the USA there is anxiety in the universities about the future of area studies. The rationale for area studies in the federal government and in other funding agencies, such as the private foundations, has already weakened. The Social Science Research Council and American Council of Learned Societies, whose work is financed by foundations such as Ford, Mellon, and Luce, has moved

---

[5] Guy J. Paulker, Frank H. Golay, Cynthia H. Enloe, *Diversity and Development in Southeast Asia: The Coming Decade* (New York: McGraw Hill, 1977), p. 91.

to abandon its area-committee structure in favor of committees that will pursue comparative and regional studies. The Councils believe that the area committees, some of which were created in the 1950s, are "not the optimum structure for providing new insights and theories suitable for a world in which the geographic units of analysis are neither static nor straightforward."[6] It is not at all clear how the new committee structure being created will exploit area studies knowledge, but we have reason to fear that the knowledge we know as area studies is being devalued and may even come to be perceived as parochial.

The "constructedness" of area studies—its funding priorities, its Eurocentric perspectives, its theoretical proclivities that may be opaque to Southeast Asians—can become the object of study in itself, to the point that it commands attention comparable to the different thought-worlds on the other side of the linguistic divide. There has been some reflection on this problem by specialists in the field. Vince Rafael, for example, has argued that Southeast Asian studies persists in maintaining the structural imbalances that conceive of the most "advanced" work taking place in the West, to which Southeast Asians must travel for their advanced degrees and enlightened understandings.[7] We may expect more scrutiny of the history and future of area studies as the funding strategies of foundations and other programs are reviewed and changed, and as area studies is forced to react and redefine itself.

New intellectual currents are also contributing to the devaluation of area studies. I am thinking here of the

---

[6] Kenneth Prewitt, "Presidential Items," *Items* (Social Science Research Council) 50.1 (March 1996): 16.

[7] Vince Raphael, "The Cultures of Area Studies in the United States," *Social Text* 41 (Winter 1994): 92–111.

fashion for, among other things, postcolonial and cultural studies. These are fields that are staking out neighboring intellectual territory. As a result, area studies are being challenged by new bodies of theory and new disciplines that make claims to knowing about other cultures. Postcolonial theory, for example, is reconfiguring what used to be called Third World or development studies. In the words of someone who has thought about postcoloniality in relation to area studies, it is a theory intended "to achieve an authentic globalization of cultural discourses by the extension globally of the intellectual concerns and orientations originating at the central sites of Euro-American cultural criticism. . . ."[8] In the postcolonial perspective colonialism is increasingly seen as something predominantly discursive, "focusing on the production of a particular cultural discourse about what is called the 'Third World' and on a certain mode of appropriation and codification of 'scholarship' and 'knowledge.'"[9] Interest in postcoloniality arises from an abiding concern for the residual effects of colonization caused by economic dependency and globalization, where the deleterious effects of overdevelopment, homogenization of culture, and the threat of extinction to local identities are understood to be the result of

---

[8] Arif Dirlik, "The Postcolonial Aura: Third World Criticism in the Age of Global Capitalism," *Critical Inquiry* 20 (Winter 1994): 329.

[9] Chandra Talpade Mohanty, "Under Western Eyes: Feminist Scholarship and Colonial Discourses," in *Colonial Discourse and Post-Colonial Theory: A Reader*, ed. and introd. Patrick Williams and Laura Chrisman (New York and Sydney: Harvester Wheatsheaf, 1993), p. 196. My use of "postcolonial" is close to Arif Dirlik's in "The Postcolonial Aura," "a description of a discourse . . . that is formed by the epistemological and psychic orientations" that are products of conditions in formerly colonial countries or global conditions after the period of colonialism.

relations of power that are similar to, if significantly different from, colonial relations of power.

With its concern for the way Western and global values and structures continue to be inscribed on the non-Western world, postcolonial theory is often expressed self-reflexively. Although she does not cite postcolonial theory, Ruth McVey would certainly include it in her list of "new modes of analysis" (postmodernism, poststructuralim, post-Marxism) that "betray the ideological exhaustion of our time."[10] The self-reflexive gaze of postcolonial theory can be so relentless that the Other, be it social system, mentality, or historical personage, is effaced, its particularities and differences obscured, although postcolonial theory makes large claims to talk about particularities and differences. In a complete reversal the phenomenological technique is sometimes taken to such extremes that to understand the Other of non-Western cultures we have to talk about *us* and these other cultures. As Anna Lowenhaupt Tsing has put it in her path-breaking ethnography, "The responses turn from the study of the Other to the study of the West, but they continue to ignore the complexity of cultural production within the interactions of colonizers and colonized."[11]

A number of scholars working on Southeast Asia avail themselves of the analytical tool kit of postcolonial theory, but it is a small number. Postcolonial theory sports very few Southeast Asianists, not a single one in a

---

[10] Ruth McVey, "Change and Continuity in Southeast Asian Studies," *Journal of Southeast Asian Studies* 26.1 (March 1995): 9.

[11] Ann Lowenhaupt Tsing, *In the Realm of the Diamond Queen: Marginality in an Out-of-the-Way Place* (Princeton: Princeton University Press, 1993): 13.

reader on the topic I recently purchased.[12] It may be that within Southeast Asia linguistic factors have in large part determined the fate of postcolonial theory in the region. If we consider that in the West postcoloniality is thriving in an Anglophonic community of scholars, it may be that English language as a medium for this theory has something to do with the (un)translatability of postcolonial terminology in Southeast Asian vernaculars. A colleague in Australia made the point to me recently that a Malay, Burmese, or Filipino would have no difficulty in understanding the postcolonial critique, unwittingly citing the three countries in which English was spoken by the colonial power. Most Southeast Asian societies retained their own languages after independence, and policies of cultural nationalism in the region have helped to maintain the use of Southeast Asian vernaculars in the school systems. The vitality of these vernaculars may account for the way all sorts of Western theory, postcolonial theory included, has been sifted and selected, accepted or rejected.

Post-colonial theory has the same limitations as other "theory" that flourishes in universities in the West. It bears the promise of applicability everywhere but turns out not to be uniformly relevant, as in the psychological impact of the colonial condition. The genealogy of this theory can be traced to the absolute dichotomies of the fierce anti-colonial thinking of Albert Memmi and Franz Fanon.[13] In my search for relevant comparative reading on the construction of the self in colonial and postcolonial history I came across such titles as *Crippled*

---

[12] Williams and Chrisman, *Colonial Discourse and Post-Colonial Theory*.

[13] Homi Bhaba, "Remembering Fanon: Self, Psyche and the Colonial Condition," in Williams and Chrisman, *Colonial Discourse and Post-Colonial Theory*, pp. 112-131

*Minds: An Exploration into Colonial Culture* (by a Sri Lankan) and *The Intimate Enemy: Loss and Recovery of Self under Colonialism* (by an Indian national).[14] For Southeast Asia one might cite as a comparable book, *Neocolonial Identity and Counter-Consciousness: Essays on Cultural Decolonization* by Renato Constantino, a work which has a very black-and-white view of the consequences of colonialism for the Philippines.[15] Constantino declares that "The basis for what developed into what is now accepted as a typically Filipino way of life and manner of viewing the world was laid during the early years of Spanish occupation," a statement that attributes present-day Filipino identity to Spanish actions in the seventeenth century.[16] On the whole, however, the psychological dimension of colonialism has not been pursued in Southeast Asian studies. Certainly "the crippled self" is not a notion that one encounters frequently in the literature on Southeast Asia, and it may be that there is something about Southeast Asia itself that resists such a notion.

But precisely because postcolonial theory has moved beyond absolute dichotomies it no longer presumes the sharp oppositions typical of the earlier period of independence movements in which Southeast Asians struggled to liberate themselves from colonial rule. About colonial societies generally it has been said that

---

[14] Susantha Goonatilake, *Crippled Minds: An Exploration into Colonial Culture* (New Delhi: Vikas Publishing House, 1982); Ashiis Nandy, *The Intimate Enemy: Loss and Recovery of Self under Colonialism* (Delhi: Oxford Univeristy Press, 1993).

[15] Renato Constantino, *Neocolonial Identity and Counter-Consciousness: Essays on Cultural Decolonization* (London: Merlin Press, 1978).

[16] Ibid., p. 32.

... colonial rule both introduced and arrested the flow of new values and institutions, and also that it both changed and froze their traditional counterparts. To say that it only subverted or froze the precolonial society is to be guilty of half-truths.[17]

In this revised view colonial societies are still seen as disrupted, but "colonialism introduced no more than one new idiom, one new strand, in the complex mosaic of the societies subjected to it."[18] Colonizing discourses did not simply destroy and depersonalize. They also generated new kinds of subjects, selves, and agents.

The idea that "colonialism introduced no more than one new idiom, one new strand" is already receiving attention in research on Southeast Asia. Keith Foulcher, the Australian literary scholar, has been engaged in studying the way the works of the Indonesian author Pramoedya Ananta Toer delve into the complex mosaic of colonial society. As Foulcher puts it, "to live in postcolonial space is to live with a sense of dispossession, and to engage in the structuring of meanings upon the dislocations that colonialism bequeaths."[19] Other scholars who have ventured into this terrain and produced new perspectives on the productivity of colonizing discourses include Ann Stoler and Aihwa Ong.[20]

---

[17] Jan Nederveen Pieterse and Bhikhu Parekh, *The Decolonization of Imagination: Culture, Knowledge and Power* (London and Atlantic Highlands: New Jersey, Zed Books Ltd., 1995), p. 2.

[18] Ibid.

[19] Keith Foulcher, "In Search of the Postcolonial in Indonesian Literature," *Sojourn* 10.2 (October 1995): 168-169.

[20] Ann Stoler, *Race and the Education of Desire: Foucault's History of Sexuality and the Colonial Order of Things* (Durham and London: Duke University Press, 1995); Aihwa Ong and Michael Peletz, eds.,

The extent to which the formulation of "no more than one new idiom, one new strand" sets an entirely new agenda is debatable. In a sense, the problematic posed by postcolonial theory is a familiar one. It arises from the dichotomies in much contemporary theory in which colonizing discourses—of knowledge, culture, economic regimes, management, strategic culture, and so forth—are set against the agency, autonomy, and self-reliance of the local.

**Postcoloniality and Selfhood**

The emergence of new kinds of subjects, selves, and agents has taken many forms. Frank Golay's work of 1969 on economic nationalism in Southeast Asia identified the assertion of an economic self. This book is a model of multi-authored scholarship, exhibiting a unity and coherence not often found in volumes of collected essays. Aside from the fact that Golay wrote half of the chapters himself, he personally put his intellectual stamp on the project by imposing a uniform structure. Each chapter deals with "the nature of indigenism" in various Southeast Asian countries: the Philippines, Indonesia, Burma, Thailand, Malaya, part of Vietnam (the south), Cambodia. Indigenism was a sign of the times, as the introduction pointed out:

> Throughout Southeast Asia the newly sovereign states sought to expand the economic functions of the public sector to include commercial, industrial, mining, and plantation enterprises. Expansion of the sector of bureaucratic enterprises obviously helps to satisfy the deep-seated urge to transfer important

---

*Bewitching Women, Pious Men: Gender and Body Politics in Southeast Asia* (Berkeley: University of California Press, 1995).

economic activities from alien to indigenous control. More important to indigenism has been the widespread use of public policies and institutions to redress handicaps that have limited participation by SEAsians in business activities.[21]

Golay saw Southeast Asian countries as willing to support public enterprise because of "the strength of socialist ideology and in all of Southeast Asia by the weakness of indigenous enterpreneurship." The operative phrase in his remarks, with its clear psychological overtones, is *"the deep-seated urge* to transfer important economic activities from alien to indigenous control."

The narrative of economic development in Southeast Asia that proceeded from this economic nationalism is not mine to tell, but suffice it to say that by the late 1980s the region was experiencing a vigorous economic dynamism. Thailand, Malaysia and Singapore enjoyed growth rates until recently of over 8 percent a year, and this economic growth has been a source of confidence. After the humiliations of the colonial period it has been empowering for the "undeveloped" or "underdeveloped" countries of Southeast Asia to become—and to be called—"economic tigers" or "Newly Industrializing Economies." Local entrepreneurship and innovation have helped to drive economic growth. This economic empowerment helps to explain how Southeast Asian leaders such as Singapore's Lee Kuan Yew and Malaysia's Prime Minister Mahathir have come to challenge what they perceive as Western hegemonic definitions of democracy, human rights, and social responsibility. The sense that Southeast Asians are in a

---

[21] Frank H. Golay et al. *Underdevelopment and Economic Nationalism in Southeast Asia* (Ithaca and London: Cornell University Press, 1969), pp. 18-19.

position to promote their own understandings of political and social life as a model for themselves and for others suggests that we should look into Southeast Asian ideas of autonomy, agency, self-reliance and self-determination, and their history.

In other words, the present Asian resurgence has a cultural as well as the overt economic dimension, and this cultural dimension is underpinned by relatively unexamined notions—or discourses—of the self. The formation and development of the nation-as-subject is much better understood, largely through mainstream studies of nationalist movements. What needs more thinking through is the construction of the subject as person-individual-citizen through this period of subject-nation-building, and the problematized connection between the two.[22]

The assertion of the self by government or bureaucracy or national leadership is generally seen to be hegemonic, something imposed, the result of elite will and management. But does this assertion of self rely entirely on elite material for its formulation or is it a more complex amalgam of subjects or selves formed "out there" in society? How were these subjects or selves "out there" formed and when? By addressing these questions, we may be able to historicize the claims that regimes make for "Asian" alternatives to previously universalized Western values. We will then be able to see these claims as part of the complex history of colonialism, postcoloniality, and modernity.

Claims of "Asian" alternatives to previously universalized Western values are not simply the product of elite imagination for the purpose of maintaining power but grow out of older movements, mentalities, and dis-

---

[22] I am indebted to Rey Ileto for helping me with this formulation.

ciplines of the self. Self-reliance and self-assertion are powerful vectors that lie behind the cultural nationalism in the region today. A decade after Indonesian independence President Sukarno gave a speech in which he called upon Indonesians "to stand on your own two feet" (*berdikari*), and thereby coined a term that entered the language. In saying this Sukarno was saying something fundamental about the trajectory of Indonesian nationalism that reached back as far as the Budi Oetomo, which "sought to revitalize the Hindu-Buddhist culture of old Java as a way of rediscovering balance, refinement, and stability lost through Westernization."[23]

But it would be a mistake to assume, simply because we think we can see the indigenous self inscribed in a practice or body of knowledge or an utterance expressing autonomy such as President Sukarno's forceful declaration, that it derives entirely from local sources. In the development literature on Thailand, for example, "local knowledge" has become something of a buzzword. The term in Thai, *phum panya*, is used in connection with the "community culture movement" that seeks to legitimate the work of Non-government Organizations (NGOs) in terms of local knowledge and networks. The term is composed of two very old words from the Buddhist lexicon (*phum* [*bhumi*], a Pali-Sanskrit word that refers to the earth, soil, or to planes of existence; and *panya*, referring to intellect or faculty of thought). Composed of old Hindu-Buddhist forms, *phum panya* or "native wisdom" has about it the whiff of antiquity, yet so far as I can discover it is a neologism, coined to concretize something important in the mentality of the moment.

---

[23] James L. Peacock, *Purifying the Faith* (Menlo Park, California: The Benjamin/Cummings Publishing Company, 1978), p. 23.

In fact, the genealogy of the Thai term for "native wisdom" or "local knowledge" has another twist in it. Though *phum panya* appears to be something that comes from within the language because of its apparently ancient pedigree, "indigenous knowledge" is also a notion that belongs to the international rhetoric of community development. In the 1950s and 1960s development rhetoric disparaged traditional knowledge as:

> inefficient, inferior, and an obstacle to development.... In reaction against Modernization Theorists and Marxists, advocates of indigenous knowledge underscore the promise it holds for agricultural production systems and sustainable development.... Indigenous knowledge is local knowledge—knowledge that is unique to a given culture or society.[24]

This reevaluation of indigenous knowledge, a knowledge that is localized in such terms as *phum panya*, means that for strategies of "development from below" to be successful they must incorporate indigenous knowledge. The populist rhetoric of indigenous knowledge seeks to empower the underprivileged and the under-represented, and it stresses the need to secure participation of indigenous groups in the process development.

*Phum panya* is thus a hybrid of global and local material. It is a discursive construct created in part by the need to claim relevance and innovative potential for development projects that might otherwise meet resistance. As such, it is a concept learned in the

---

[24] Arun Agrawal, "Dismantling the Divide Between Indigenous and Scientific Knowledge," *Development and Change* 26, 3 (July 1995): 413–14. I am indebted to Professor Tessa Morris-Suzuki for first suggesting that I look for local knowledge in the international rhetoric of development, and to Dr. Aat Vervoorn for this helpful citation.

international language of development. As a keyword that appears to be coming from within the language even as it has been translated from the outside, *phum panya* is similar to other famous coinages in Southeast Asian history such as god-king, in ancient Khmer history (*devaraja*), which carry the cachet of foreign prestige as well as the authenticity of the local.

## Southeast Asian Selfhood: Suggestions for Further Inquiry

On the practical question of the kind of inquiry I think would be fruitful for study of the self in Southeast Asia, I would suggest that we look across the region and note some of the common features in twentieth-century history. The historical literature on this topic is uneven—strong for some parts of the region, weak for others. Most of the work on the period leading up to independence is typically concerned with organizations and their roles in nationalist movements. Interest in untangling the emerging notions of self and personhood has generally been stimulated by nationalism rather than by a desire to understand the prehistory of these notions. I can suggest three areas that would be productive for thinking about the problem. Needless to say, these areas overlap, and to a certain extent they require study by different disciplines. But they would also benefit from interdisciplinary treatment, and it is in the spirit of that I outline them here.

1) *Literary production*. In the late colonial and early postcolonial periods writers were concerned to tell stories about the paradoxes and dilemmas facing the self in its nationalist awakening. In an important article Benedict Anderson remarked on the obscurity of the transformation of consciousness in early Indonesian nationalist thinking. He specifically referred to the Budi

Utomo, the early nationalist organization whose foundation day of May 20, 1908 is celebrated in Indonesia as the Day of National Awakening.[25] For most of Southeast Asia the transformation of consciousness continues to remain obscure. This important dimension of the region's twentieth-century history is altogether missing from the latest codification in English of Southeast Asian historiography, the *Cambridge History of Southeast Asia*, which unaccountably omits discussion of even the most prominent literary developments.[26]

To rectify historiography's failure to come to terms with this transformation of consciousness, Anderson puzzled over the form and language of the "autobiography" of R. Soetomo, the Javanese founder of Budi Utomo. Essentially he offered a nuanced reading of the "autobiography," tracing the emergence of a new "watching self" that was evidence of a distancing between person and culture. This "watching self," acutely aware of the racial injustices of colonial society, was called into existence by those injustices, and coexisted with the inner self (*bathin*) that was deeply Javanese. Soetomo's awakening (*kesadaran* or awareness, says Anderson, is *the* key word of early nationalist thought) consists, in part, of his growing awareness of his own Javaneseness. Soetomo in his maturity and awakening grew closer to ancestral qualities: "The quest is not for individual fulfillment or historical uniqueness,

---

[25] Benedict R. O'G. Anderson, "A Time of Darkness and a Time of Light: Transposition in Early Indonesian Nationalist Thought," in his *Language and Power: Exploring Political Cultures in Indonesia* (Ithaca: Cornell University Press, 1990), p. 245.

[26] Nicholas Tarling, ed. *The Cambridge History of Southeast Asia*, vol. 2, *The Nineteenth and Twentieth Centuries* (Cambridge: Cambridge University Press, 1992).

but for reunion and identification."[27] It is as if discovery of what it meant to be Javanese was necessary if Soetomo was to move towards Indonesian-ness.

The ambiguities of connection with and separation from the past, such as Anderson observed in Soetomo's thought-world, are to be found in other literary traditions in the region. Literary historians working on Thai, Malay, and Vietnamese literature from the 1920s to the 1950s have turned their attention to the types of selves being written into those literatures, especially in the novel. Notions of manhood and womanhood were created and questioned in this literature and debated in magazines and the press. In Thailand the woman-as-exemplar-of-progress and the woman-as-warrior were fashioned out of older historical material.[28] There were distinctly nationalist strains in these constructions of personhood. The martial motif, for example, fed into a larger narrative about Siam's ability to stand against Western imperialism, a narrative that was exploited by the militarists who came to power in the late 1930s. These constructions of womanhood entered into the debates about social change and attitudes towards polygamy that led to the overthrow of the absolute monarchy in 1932. Such conceptions of the self played an enormous role in the formation of Siam's public culture during the 1930s and must ultimately be seen to be more important in the political history of the period than is conventionally portrayed.

In Vietnam, "the new generation of literary artists that came of age in the early 1930s expressed an intensely personal point of view with great passion. . . .

---

[27] Ibid., p. 249.

[28] Scot Barmé, "Talking Women: Early Twentieth Century Discourses on Women in Siam," in Nerida Cook and Peter Jackson, eds., *Gender and Sexuality in Modern Thailand*, forthcoming.

This was a process of collective reorientation, a quest for some new and urgently needed sense of dignity and self-worth."[29] These literary works followed by only a few decades the period when Vietnamese intellectuals looked to Chinese translations of Western thinkers such as Rousseau, Voltaire, Montesquieu, Darwin, and Herbert Spencer coming out of the "'self-strengthening' movement in China."[30]

In his valuable discussion of this current in Vietnamese literary history Neil Jamieson tends to use the language of the psychodymanics of self-development and self-creation, but elsewhere he elucidates the transformation of consciousness with a more social analysis. In the early 1930s some of these Vietnamese literary artists formed themselves into the Self-Strength (or Self-Reliant) Literary Group. They attacked oppressive and corrupt social institutions, sometimes focusing their criticism on the Vietnamese family itself and what had been called the "family mentality," "the prison of family life that was the bulwark of the oppressive social structure they had to over-throw if their ideals were to be realized."[31] They did this by championing the freedom of the individual through what Greg Lockhart has called "I" narratives, in which the writer's consciousness has become externalized.[32] This emergent personhood privileged "nonpersons," the ordinary folk without power or status who were thought of as more "authentic, alive, and aware" in their challenging the decadence and

---

[29] Neil L. Jamieson, *Understanding Vietnam* (Berkeley: University of California Press, 1993), p. 103.

[30] Ibid., p. 57.

[31] Ibid., pp. 154–155.

[32] Greg Lockhart, trans. and introd., "Broken Journey: Nhat Linh's 'Going to France,'" *East Asian History* 8 (December 1995): 73–134.

irrationality of colonial society.³³ The debate the writers of the Self-Strength Literary Group engendered was emblematic of—and contributed to—the polarization over the definition of personhood that was taking place in Vietnamese society more generally. In privileging the individual, the Self-Strength Literary Group also drew criticism for "glorifying selfishness."

A comparable debate about literature, the individual, and society occupied Malay writers in the 1950s. In discussing this debate, Virginia Hooker has pointed out that a comparison of the Malay ASAS 50 group (Generation of the 1950s Group) and the 1950s literary movement in Indonesia exemplified by LEKRA (The People's Institute of Culture) is a comparison begging to be made.³⁴ A comparison is also begging to be made here with the Vietnamese Self-Strength Literary Group as well as with the Thai "Art for Life, Art for the People" groups of the 1950s.³⁵ Similar polarizations over the definition of personhood are to be found in all these cases.

The hallmark of ASAS 50 in Malay literature was a push in favor of art for society, as against the individual. Expressions of "self" would not be helpful in the process of modernization and progress, it was argued by these literati, as such expressions would not be understood by the people. The group characterized literature

---

[33] Jamieson, *Understanding Vietnam*, pp 156–157.

[34] Virginia Matheson Hooker, "Developing a Rhetoric for Malay Society," *Jurnal Persuraton Melayu* 8.2 (1995): 50.

[35] The Art for Life, Art for the People movement in Thailand, which occurred synchronously with ASAS 50 in postcolonial Malaya, was fueled by an intense interest in social realism inspired by Soviet and Chinese translations. See Craig J. Reynolds, *Thai Radical Discourse: The Real Face of Thai Feudalism Today* (Ithaca: Cornell Southeast Asia Program, 1994; Reprint Edition), pp. 25–26.

that stressed individual initiative as "egotistical, subjective, and useless to the *rakyat* (people). . . . Such a system of values equates individualism with selfishness and self-indulgence."[36] The Generation of the 1950s had difficulty locating its readership, because a *rakyat* audience did not exist at that time, but the Group bequeathed a legacy to later generations by questioning the place of individuality in the progress of society. Here, self-strengthening must be understood as the strengthening of a collectivity—the people, the *rakyat*—that was more inclusive than an individual self.

What is not well understood in the transformation of the self in modern Southeast Asian literary traditions is the connection between the modern self and older notions of self-cultivation and self-development. Here it is useful to recall Anderson's essay on Soetomo and the literal translation of *budi utama* as "perfected moral faculty." The older notion of perfection was necessarily changed in new contexts and now contained a sense of ethical commitment.

2) *Religious reform movements.* Many Southeast Asian societies have long encouraged practices, including meditation, for controlling the body's desires and avoiding conflict. These practices, a form of cultivation of the self that is documented in the oldest historical materials, lead to higher spiritual attainments. Such practices shape Southeast Asian hierarchies as well as institutions and are embedded in technological processes. In early Southeast Asia, for example, it has been suggested that metal-working technology serves as a kind of metaphor of spiritual transmutation. Stanley O'Connor's analysis of a hitherto indecipherable

---

[36] Hooker, "Developing a Rhetoric for Malay Society," p. 52. This appeal to the *rakyat* is highly inflected by ethnicity, as *rakyat* refers only to ethnic Malays.

sculpture in a fifteenth-century mountain sanctuary in Central Java demonstrates the isomorphism between metallurgy and the liberation of the soul. In the fashioning of krises and other metal objects the blacksmith performs operations that parallel the transformation of the human body as it metamorphizes from its putrefied state in death to liberation and deliverance.[37]

The rapid socio-economic changes of the late twentieth century have brought transformations of these practices both at the individual level and at the community level. In some cases "reform" religious practices are designed to protect the self from the unwanted effects of modernity—a stay against confusion, disorder, and upheaval. In other cases these movements have developed ways of confronting the effects of modernity, seeing new opportunities in modernity. Intensive ascetic training, for example, can lead to greater decisiveness, mental clarity, and peace of mind, all of which are useful in making business decisions and furthering the growth of the Southeast Asian economic tigers.

In referring to the transformation of consciousness at the community level, I have in mind the so-called political-religious sects of southern Vietnam (Hoa Hao, Cao Dai), the Buddhist reform movements in Thailand (Bupphasawan, Wat Thammakai), and the Muhammadijah movement in Indonesia. Each of these movements in its own way demonstrates the points I have been making, but I want to mention specifically the Muhammadijah, the reformist Islamic movement founded in 1912 in Jogjakarta. In its rediscovery of an older identity as a way of responding to the pressures and alienation of change, it exhibits the interplay between present

---

[37] Stanley J. O'Connor, "Metallurgy and Immortality at Candi Sukuh, Central Java," *Indonesia* 39 (April 1985): 53–70.

and past I have been discussing.[38] The Muhammadijah has concentrated on evangelism, welfare, and education by following the methodical and rational program of its founder, Kijai Hadji Achmad Dahlan. Its leadership has stayed away from politics and has been regarded as one of the most selfless and least corrupt of any major Indonesia-based organization. With its programs of schools and training camps it instills in members a sense of collective struggle and evangelism for the sake of the movement. Members are encouraged to practice ethics and cultivate a distilled spirit (*tauhid*) in order to control earthly drives.

3) *Disciplines of the body*. The importance of mental and physical discipline in these religious movements, such as the cultivation of the *tauhid* in the Muhammadijah, brings me to the last examples of the transformation of self, namely, disciplines of the body. Much remains to be studied and said about the relationship between disciplines of the body (cultivation of the physical self) and authoritarian government that has been a feature of postcolonial Southeast Asia. In terms of physical culture, the Boy Scout movement is important in many of the region's nationalisms. Strong, healthy bodies make strong, healthy nations; the discipline and health of the body are essential to good citizenship.

Apart from physical culture, one could also point to ascesis, trance, and invulnerability practices. I mention ascesis, because disciplining the mind also involves disciplining the body; the two are inseparable in many Southeast Asian religious practices. In Theravada Buddhism one strengthens oneself by purging the mind of

---

[38] James L. Peacock, *Purifying the Faith*, p. 23. See also Alfian, *Muhammadiyah: The Political Behavior of a Muslim Modernist Organization under Dutch Colonialism* (Yogyakarta: Gadjah Mada University Press, 1989).

defilements. Southeast Asian concepts of potency stem from practices that lead to selflessness and thereby to greater control and order. In trance, which is a form of discipline of the body, heroes from the past—sometimes distinct historical figures—are reincarnated. Rituals to instill invulnerability in practitioners is widespread throughout the region. In Thailand the cultivation and practice of invulnerability is seen to be a "valuable kind of knowledge buried deep in the veins of [us] Thai people since ancient times."[39] Knowledge of invulnerability, an ancient knowledge that commands respectability because of its antiquity, was deployed by Thai soldiers in wars against the Lao and Vietnamese in the early nineteenth century and later by soldiers in the Second World War, in Korea and Indochina.

Is there a connection between these disciplines of the body, either ascesis, invulnerability practices, or the physical culture used in the training sessions of reformist religious groups, and authoritarian rule? Militarism in the twentieth century tends to be explained by the weakness of parliamentary forms, by the ease with which national liberation armies appropriated the bureaucratic forms and institutional ambitions of the colonial state. But could it not be that militarism also owes something to the array of disciplinary practices of the body by which men (and, in some cases, women) sought to protect themselves in dangerous and frightening situations? The success of one of Thailand's most popular politicians in recent years, Chamlong Srimuang, has partly to do with the fact that his reputation for meditational practice *and* his career in the army, where he rose to the rank of major

---

[39] Andrew Turton, "Invulnerability and Local Knowledge," in Manas Chitakasem and Andrew Turton, eds., *Thai Constructions of Knowledge* (London: University of London, School of Oriental and African Studies, 1991), p. 166.

general, tapped something deep in the Thai character and Thai culture that valued these qualities on a personal level. The strength of older disciplinary practices of the body might explain the kind of national self championed by military governments in the postcolonial period.

## Conclusion

I began this discussion with the broad issue of self-determination at the national level, an issue that helped to define the direction and scope of Southeast Asian area studies. I then suggested how recent academic theory, which makes claims for studying relations of power, has had an impact on area studies. I did this in order to indicate the larger modernist project in which the field of Southeast Asian studies is embedded, as we can see in the way the "autonomous history" of Southeast Asia paradigm has been used to legitimate and empower both Southeast Asia as well as Southeast Asian studies.[40] This regnant paradigm is clearly visible in the work of Frank Golay, where I found inspiration for what I wanted to say about twentieth-century history.

I then related Southeast Asian assertiveness that comes from economic prowess to the cultural domain and posed some questions, suggesting that it would be misleading to ascribe local agency entirely to purely Southeast Asian forms. So complex and entangled is the modern self in Southeast Asia that the quest for authentic, wholly indigenous Southeast Asian selves must be perpetually frustrated.[41] But it is important to address how an emerging and new sense of "self," both

---

[40] I argued for this connection in "A New Look at Old Southeast Asia," *Journal of Asian Studies* 54,2 (May 1995): 419–446.

[41] See my "Authenticating Southeast Asia in the Absence of Colonialism," *Asian Studies Review* 15,3 (April 1992): 141–151.

individual and collective, is taking shape in Southeast Asia.

Finally, I delineated three areas where I suggested it might be promising to think about the formation of the modern self in Southeast Asia in light of older discourses about the self. These areas are literary production, religious movements and disciplines of the body. In the vigorous dialectical relationship between the modern transformation of the self and these older discourses the self is problematized and the boundaries of the self questioned.

I have advocated a comparative framework for thinking about the problems, because I believe there will be intellectual benefit. Once we look beyond the big "-isms" of the twentieth century—nationalism, religious reformism, militarism, and so forth—the comparative framework for modern Southeast Asian historical studies is still very weak.

We may think we understand the history of political self-determination in Southeast Asia, but the cultural dimensions of self-determination are not so well understood. The assertion of national identity by cultural means is not just statist and elitist but draws on—and argues with—more popular notions of the self. These notions of self originate in "society" and circulate in popular culture where they draw on premodern discourses of self. National leaders, institutions, and regimes are usually seen as exploiting rather than embodying notions of personhood. But the notions of self that the elite employ are not totally divorced from popular notions that are often viewed as primordial and residual, to be "developed" and transformed in the effort to achieve "modernity."

I am not for a minute satisfied with the vocabulary I have used—personhood, self, self-determination, self-cultivation. But I propose that in this cluster of values and practices there is opportunity for area studies, now being pressured by theory as much as by a transformed Southeast Asia, to find new orientations and lines of inquiry.

# GLOBALIZATION, MARGINALIZATION, AND THE STUDY OF SOUTHEAST ASIA

## Ruth McVey[1]

The problem I should like to address is why, when in the last few decades Southeast Asia has become increasingly globalized, Southeast Asian studies is being marginalized as a field of academic attention in the United States.

By "globalization" here I mean the region's appearing more prominently in general perception through its

---

[1] The writing and revision of this lecture have been made easier by the generous advice and criticism of many people. I should particularly like to thank Barbara Harvey, Thomas Kirsch, Craig Reynolds, Heather Sutherland, and Oliver Wolters for their suggestions and also Singapore's Institute for Southeast Asian Studies for providing a congenial and stimulating environment for the re-writing. Needless to say, the mistakes are mine.

involvement in an increasingly dense international web of communications, trade, tourism, politics, economic activity, and consumer culture. Above all, Southeast Asia has achieved recent notice as part of the Asian-Pacific "economic miracle," and attention has focused on its countries as lessons in capitalist achievement. While in an earlier day people who studied about Southeast Asia had to confront the argument that it wasn't a "real" region but an artificial category based on geographic propinquity, Southeast Asians themselves have been giving it a perceptual and institutional reality through ASEAN and other, so far mostly governmental and economic, forms of cooperation. In such ways Southeast Asia appears both more real and more relevant to our lives; why not then Southeast Asian studies? For there seems to be a general perception among American scholars I've talked to, or whose comments I've read, that the study of Southeast Asia is on the defensive both in terms of intellectual attention and institutional support, that it is becoming marginalized as a field of academic attention.

This is not, I think, because of some failing intrinsic to Southeast Asian studies itself but rather because the field is part of that scholarly approach called "area studies," nearly all branches of which have been experiencing hard times. Financial reasons for this have often been pointed out: the general contraction of academic funding has hit particularly hard at programs that demand long training, expensive library investment, and funds for field work. But, more important I think, there has also been a significant intellectual rethinking which has led scholarly interest and funding priorities away from area studies.

On the face of it, this is odd. After all, there is now a greater general appreciation of the importance of the world beyond North America and Europe, and of the need to learn from—not just study about—the experience of non-Western societies. "Globalization" is the recent buzz word; why not therefore the study of other parts of the globe? There has also been increasing scholarly talk of the need for analysis to be both multicultural and multidisciplinary (or transdisciplinary). Area studies aims to be both these things, so we might expect it to be at the center rather than the fringes of the recent intellectual movement. But, with the exception of works by a few individual scholars,[2] this has not been the case. Certainly there has been no general academic perception that area studies has anything to contribute to the effort to transcend the boundaries of discipline and the parochialism of cultural assumptions. In order to see why this is so, and to consider its implications for the study of Southeast Asia, I think we need to look at how the area studies approach developed, to discover the intellectual assumptions behind it, and to ask whether they still illuminate the problems of our time. If they don't, can we usefully revise them, or should we allow the field of area studies to continue its recession towards the margins of scholarly activity?

"Area studies" as an academic field was developed in the US after World War II, but it had earlier ancestors in the training programs for colonial administrators and advisers that were set up in European universities from around the beginning of this century. These aimed primarily at producing "language officers" who had a systematic knowledge of the customs, religion, and

---

[2] For Southeast Asia studies these are most famous: Clifford Geertz, Benedict Anderson, and James C. Scott. I can think of perhaps a dozen others who have had an impact on other disciplines and areas, but most students of Southeast Asia have either remained within the intellectual bounds of the region or moved out of area studies entirely.

indigenous power structures of the places they were to administer. They were not just dedicated "training courses" but multidisciplinary programs designed to give a broader understanding of the people and cultures being studied. As such, they did both more and less than what was intended by their government and business sponsors.

One source of their deviation from imperial sponsors' purposes arose precisely because of their being *too* "relevant"—that is, too involved in the questions of the day. Knowledge of and sympathy for the area of study might combine with idealistic commitment to render the scholar unavailable or unreliable for imperial purposes. We can thus see that, while there was by no means the tension between government and academe or the questioning of imperialism that took place in the postwar US, questions of "relevance" vs "true scholarship" were already there, and arguments over whether the area expert should give precedence to the requirements of patrons or the interests of the people studied, or should strive for a state of scholarly disinterestedness.

While the argument over political position seems familiar to later American experience, the second major source of prewar deviation from sponsors' requirements appears to be very different—though, as we shall eventually see, it is not entirely without relevance to the present situation. This second influence was Orientalism. Edward Said and others have shown how the Orientalist approach served imperial purposes, but we should also consider the degree to which Orientalism turned academic eyes *away* from colonial interests. After all, it withdrew scholarly skills and attention from the "real" problems of colonial rule and economic extraction in favor of immersion in exotic high cultures, preferably long-dead ones.

One reason for scholars to turn to Orientalism was, no doubt, to escape the unpleasant consequences of offending the established powers with wrong opinions on "relevant" subjects; but very likely that was a minor consideration. Rather, it appealed because it fit into the philological tradition that was still powerful in European universities at the beginning of the century, and was thus linked to a tradition of study aimed at finding the roots of civilization. It was thus high-status and also arcane, both desiderata in academe. Orientalism said that relevant knowledge was not something you could acquire by, say, living in a place and observing what went on there, or by applying techniques you had learned from general university study.

The scholar specializing on Southeast Asia was thus not just a "resource person" for business and administrative interests; rather, he possessed a special, secret knowledge without which attempts at the solution of contemporary problems would be superficial and temporary. If government or business appealed to him, the Orientalist might condescend to remove his gaze from the more profound spheres of civilizational understanding and advise (as many Orientalists did) on a culturally appropriate line of approach to immediate problems of empire; but he advised from on high, as squalid contemporary issues were not his concern. This satisfyingly reversed the scholar-sponsor relationship implicit in the "language-officer" approach to foreign parts, asserting the brahman's superiority over the king. It did this, ultimately, at the expense of making bureaucratic and business patrons wonder whether they were getting their money's worth out of scholarship.

The post World War II development of area studies in the US both contrasted with and continued the prewar European experience. On the face of it, the contradiction is most apparent: the US emphasized "Asian studies" rather than Oriental studies, modernity as a universal goal, national liberation rather than colonial administration, social sciences rather than language and history. It was assumed that US and new-nation interests converged through "development." Modernization and democratization were assumed to go hand in hand. Southeast Asia, as a "new" area, fit unambiguously into this framework, and the Cornell Southeast Asia Program in its early years epitomized this approach. Nonetheless, certain intellectual assumptions remained the same, or at least were strikingly similar. One was that the region was basically a terra incognita, which could only be understood through appropriately trained outsiders. Another, related, was the assumption that the purpose of scholarship was to fit the "facts" of the new countries' circumstances into a framework conceived for them from abroad, and ultimately to guide them in a direction congenial to the western powers. What was demanded of the new Southeast Asia experts was "country knowledge." Politics, anthropology, economics, and subjects related to development were appropriate major fields. History was pertinent insofar as it related to the struggle for independence and modernity. Language (understood as the national language) was an important tool, but only that: the US had no philological tradition, and "Orientalism" was seen both as irrelevant and ideologically suspect. Literature, art, etc. were cultural frills, useful merely to understand better contemporary popular attitudes, especially towards the great issues of modernization and national unity.

This approach tended to produce scholars with multidisciplinary but highly focused knowledge, engaged with the problems of the day. Such specialists generally had a strong disciplinary background—"Asian

Studies" and other non-disciplinary degrees proved too intellectually unfocused and devoid of employment possibilities above the MA level—but they rarely entered the mainstream of discussion within their disciplines. Rather (with the partial exception of anthropology), Southeast Asia specialists tended to talk to each other, or to bureaucratic specialists in the region, and not to non-experts on the area, or even scholars engaged in studying other "non-western" societies. If their research findings challenged general assumptions within the discipline this was usually discovered, if at all, by generalists who stumbled by accident across their writings. This was not due so much to Southeast Asian specialists' scholarly modesty as (at least in the heyday of area studies) to a feeling of overriding commitment to Southeast Asia as a focus of interest, combined with a belief that "conventional" disciplinary concerns were peripheral not only to their area of interest but to the real issues facing the world, which centered on the emergence of new nations and their achievement of modernity.

This concentration produced a good deal of very distinguished studies, whose enduring value is evident today. Frank Golay's work epitomized this tradition, in its concrete but analytical treatment of the great issues of economic development and national identity. In the first lecture of this series, Eric Thorbecke demonstrated the virtues of the approach, in a consideration of the political economy of development in Indonesia and the Philippines which took off from Golay's propositions. His discussion addressed issues of contemporary relevance, which had useful policy implications, and which also made points of theoretical import; and it made no attempt to exalt its message by mystifying it.

But if this "classical" American approach to Southeast Asia has its virtues, it has also had its drawbacks. For one thing, its exaltation of area over discipline made it easy—indeed, a pleasure—for those not involved in area studies to ignore or ghettoize them once regional studies had ceased to be the darling of the grant-givers. For another, graduate students in the field were programmed to believe that, once they had got teaching jobs, they should aim at least to teach a course on Southeast Asia and ultimately to establish an area-focused collectivity. Teaching non-area courses was a chore which diverted the Southeast Asianist from his "real" work. This made for tension between discipline and area specialists in departments—only anthropology, which had made the integration of theory and local observation a central disciplinary concern, seemed able to avoid this—and caused much frustration among Southeast Asianists seeking employment when area studies ceased to expand.

The golden age of Southeast Asia studies, and area studies generally in American universities, was the 1950s and 1960s, when modernization and western-style democracy were still unquestioned as civilizational goals, the interests of the US and the "third world" were still seen as congruent, and expert knowledge of the new Southeast Asian nations seemed the key to insuring the intermeshing of these elements. But already by the mid-60s these assumptions were being questioned, particularly the compatibility of US and third-world interests; for Southeast Asianists, the Vietnam War made this all too relevant. Funds dried up as government came to see academic area specialists as a source of criticism more than support, and as foundations sought to avoid charges of funding imperialism (or communism) by discovering urgent issues of poverty and injustice at home. This dealt a heavy blow to Southeast Asian and other area studies, but in a way it was superficial—the breaks of the patronage game, which might change. Far more important has been a general intellectual disenchantment with modernization and national self-realization as universal goals, a retreat which began in the 1970s and has left not only area studies but also many of the disciplines without a sense of direction.

Increasingly, in the last two decades, the methodological forefront of academic studies has been occupied by the "posts"—post-modernism, post-structuralism, post-colonialism and so on. The labels themselves reflect the loss of old paradigms and the failure to find a new intellectual framework. This disenchantment led to a variety of attempts at "deconstructing" and "unpacking" established ways of thought, and eventually the development of "disciplinarity," a whole new branch of scholarly navel-gazing. We can see the effects of this loss of certainty in the second of the Golay lectures, Craig Reynolds's discussion of "Self-Cultivation and Self-Determination in Postcolonial Southeast Asia." Concerned not with structure but with perception and experience, it seeks to uncover the cultural and political assumptions behind our approaches to Southeast Asia as well as Southeast Asians' approaches to themselves.

The impulse towards introspection created by the postmodern questioning of assumptions can easily lead away from rather than towards cultural openness through its tendency to transform all queries into reflections on our inner selves. Distant times, exotic cultures, and marginal groups are thus taken as instances of Otherness by means of which we can distinguish the outlines of our own civilization. This has led to intellectually exciting but also esoteric studies, which often employ a vocabulary accessible only to scholarly adepts. As with European Orientalism, it satisfies the academic urge to demonstrate mastery of the arcane, but it also raises the question of the wider relevance of such scholarship for understanding Southeast Asia.

This said, the self-questioning of the post-modernist approach is something to be cherished, for it grants us a rare opportunity to be aware of the limits of our common assumptions and to attempt to formulate something new. Its preference for marginal and distant aspects of society arises not simply from an impulse towards the arcane but from the desire to escape the old area studies fixation on nation and development. Thus it both undermines the ideological assumptions of conventional area studies and beckons us on new paths towards understanding.[3]

At the same time that postmodernist studies have attacked area studies from (usually) the local level, globalism has attacked it from above. As Arif Dirlik has argued, the increasing emphasis on supranational relationships reflects the change from a period characterized by the cold war and a US-European-dominated pattern of capitalist development to one where the west is no longer challenged ideologically but also no longer seems the *sine qua non* of capitalism. The new era is characterized by world economic rather than political competition, by communications and information technology rather than manufacturing strength, by transnational corporations and mobile labor forces, and by the pervasive penetration of "modern" education, discourse, and consumer culture.[4] Nation-states now

---

[3] For an excellent study of such re-thinking, see John R. Bowen, "The Forms Culture Takes: A State-of-the-Field Essay on the Anthropology of Southeast Asia," *Journal of Asian Studies* 54 (1995): 1047-1078.

[4] Arif Dirlik, "No Longer Far Away: The Reconfiguration of Global Relations and Its Challenge to Asian Studies." Paper delivered to the Center for Asian Studies, University of Amsterdam, October 8, 1996.

exist in a network of political, economic, and social relations which extend beyond their borders and erode their sovereignty; populations and ideas have an unprecedented mobility, and the whole world seems simultaneously more standardized and more heterogeneous.

The new globalist perspective reflects this change by downplaying the centrality of nations, in the process denying a basic assumption of conventional area studies. Its concerns are, if not literally global, at least of a scope that transcends national boundaries. The particularities of place are acknowledged in the proclaimed need for "context sensitivity," but often such input is declared best left to "globally acculturated" informants from the area concerned, whose understanding of their own societies is taken for granted. In other words, there is no longer a real need for the non-native area specialist and thus for area studies.

The new globalism, as Dirlik points out, is to a considerable extent a repackaging of an ideological and economic hegemony previously identified with the west, so as to make it appear universal and inevitable. It thus avoids the no longer tenable insistence on a western-style road to capitalism, while at the same time it denies the possibility of any real alternative experience.

Moreover, though the ever-thickening web of global economic, cultural, political, and technological connections is bringing about a marked homogeneity of manners and perspectives, this standardization is as superficial as it is real. Where developmentalism sought to translate all local experience into episodes in the self-realization of the nation-state, globalism simply ignores indigenous understandings. The shared assumptions which it reflects are, for the most part, those of a relatively wealthy upper layer of society, which finds it both easy and profitable to interact with its international counterparts. In the process of fitting into the global discourse, such an elite may lose what connection it had with the thinking of the rest of society. The proposal that context sensitivity be obtained by consulting globally acculturated native informants thus runs the very real danger that these interlocutors may have little idea of what ordinary people are thinking or who they look to for leadership. It is of course no new thing for international experts to agree on the nature of a problem only to find that their proposed solutions cannot be implemented in the countries they "represent" because their own meeting of minds had little to do with local perceptions. With globalization this threatens to become a massive systemic problem.

The paragons and pioneers of the global approach have been the great multinational corporations, and not surprisingly their thinking has had a profound influence on the foundations which depend on their largesse and which are in turn the principal source of training and research grants for area studies. The result has been a radical reduction in foundation support, with financial resources being channeled instead into projects which deny, or at least drastically downplay, the importance of local knowledge.[5]

---

[5] One of the last significant sources of funding for area studies training and research was the Social Science Research Council; for a statement arguing for a redirection of its support see Stanley J. Heginbotham, "Rethinking International Scholarship: The Challenge of Transition from the Cold War Era," *Items* 48, 2-3 (1994): 33-40; and issues of that publication for 1995 and 1996 for the steps which accomplished this.

But at the same time that the global approach poses a threat to area studies, it also grants it a great opportunity. Like postmodern studies, globalism performs the signal service of attacking the field's fixation with the nation-state. Moreover, while at one level globalism may repackage an old capitalist hegemony, at another it reflects contemporary social transformations that will have consequences of their own. The issues which its advocates have stressed—urbanization, political economy, the lifestyle of the new elites, environmental problems, transfers of knowledge, and the transformation of the working force—are very real and are urgently in need of attention by centers of Southeast Asia studies. Finally, the ideological homogenization and stratification implied by globalism is a thesis pursued hotly by its antithesis of NGOs, ethnonationalisms, and other antihegemonic transnational movements. Hence globalization as a process must be taken most seriously if we are to understand Southeast Asia today.

In postmodernism and globalism, area studies thus confront two intellectual trends which deny their conventional assumptions but in the process offer them the possibility of transcending their present limitations. However, we also need to ask at this point whether we should bother at all to rescue the approach. Would it not make more sense to say that area-based fields have had their day, and that studies of Southeast Asia should simply be absorbed into the disciplines or into some general comparative approach? This argument has recently been quite popular among funding organizations, not least because it provides a justification for eliminating what remains of their support for area programs.

However, this nostrum won't work. It assumes both that the disciplines will become more open to other cultures—and indeed to their fellow disciplines—and that the problem of the lengthy immersion needed to acquire adequate local knowledge can be finessed by addressing one's self to particular problems rather than by securing a general background. If you deal, say, with the question of preserving rainforests and wish to consider the Indonesian case, do you really need to know how Indonesian politics works, or how the economy functions, or how local communities are organized and what they believe? Indeed you do, if you hope to formulate a sensible response to the problem. If you don't know the political interests involved in timber concessions, the economic and social role of swidden cultivation, and the interplay of local ethnicities, you will at best come up with an irrelevant recommendation and at worst with a recipe for disaster. "Context-sensitivity" can't be acquired on the cheap.

As has been unkindly but accurately pointed out, the academic disciplines themselves are a form of European/North American area studies, and (outside of anthropology, whose business it is to deal with such things), they have shown little interest in other parts of the world. Their tendency, in the face of increasing financial stringency and the proliferation of specializations, has been to insist on the (Euroamerican) basics and/or the latest theoretical fashions. The new emphasis on multidisciplinarity (or transdisciplinarity) very often involves the "raiding" of one discipline by another, by applying superficially acquired techniques of another discipline to a problem investigated in one's own. (History has been a special victim of this, a latter-day instance, perhaps, of its being too important to leave to historians).⁶ All this leaves little place for the local groundedness necessary to understanding very different cultures and historical experiences.

Yet it is precisely such a groundedness in local understanding that can offer postmodernism protection against the introversion that threatens its accessibility, globalism a shield against the superficiality and irrelevance that often accompany its generalizations, and that can bring a real universality to the disciplines. Moreover, the fact that Southeast Asia encompasses a number of cultures which are quite different and yet have certain geographical, historical, and cultural characteristics in common provides the basis for manageable and useful comparative study. The possibility of being both comparative *and* multidisciplinary, having both flexibility and a focal point, is an major advantage for contemporary intellectual exploration. This is what Southeast Asia studies really has to offer, and it would be throwing the baby out with the bathwater to get rid of the approach simply because of the limitations of its past practice. Area specialization is if anything more necessary than ever, to correct and refine the new intellectual approaches and to provide a deeper comprehension of our increasingly close-knit world.

It cannot do so, however, if Southeast Asia studies continues to be conceived in its original form. The idea that we have to train pools of specialists who know a lot

---

⁶ For a good discussion of this, in the context of a European academic environment, see Heather Sutherland, "Writing Indonesian History in the Netherlands," *Bijdragen tot de taal-, land- en volkenkunde* 150, 5 (1994): 785-804. A similar point has been made concerning the ubiquitous contemporary emphasis on culture; see Tessa Morris-Suzuki, "The Invention and Reinvention of 'Japanese Culture,'" *Journal of Asian Studies* 54 (1995): 760.

about a specific area and are therefore an important national resource is not compelling to post-cold-war patrons. The field is now a relatively mature one; there is generally enough literature for basic area knowledge to be available to non-area experts (rather, the problem now is how to order the great flood of material we have). Moreover, the spread of elite knowledge of English, the ease of travel to Southeast Asia, and the westernization of institutions in the major cities of the region make the role of the academic area specialist as interpreter seem less essential to the present-day decision-maker and program-funder. Indeed, as the globalists are happy to point out, it is quite likely that the American businessman or technical expert will understand a Southeast Asian counterpart far more readily than he will a US academic explaining Southeast Asia in postmodernist terms. We need to re-think our approach to Southeast Asian studies—we won't get very far by simply asserting defensively that the field *is* multidisciplinary and multicultural and *must* therefore be up-to-date. We must make it so, must reinvent it; and the obstacles that must be overcome are mental and organizational even more than financial.

An essential element in re-thinking Southeast Asian studies (or any regionally-based study) is to make clear what we mean by the "area" in area studies. Too often it is simply a space on a map, demarcated by a national boundary or series of national boundaries, about which knowledge is to be acquired. This was indeed the concept in the cold-war beginnings of the field, and it is one of the reasons why it now seems old-fashioned. Perhaps a simple name-change is called for, but I think it is also important to make clearer what the focus needs to be (and indeed always was for the field's best practitioners).

What we must be concerned with is not geopolitical space but the people who share a particular (but not rigidly demarcated) part of the world. Their histories, cultures, and environments may intertwine and come apart over time; depending on what aspect we study, a space far smaller or far wider than regional or national boundaries may be relevant, but what matters are patterns of human conditions, perceptions, and experience. It is not that Southeast Asia is the object of our study, but that Southeast Asians are its subject.

Southeast Asia specialists also need to do more to justify their claims to being multi-disciplinary and cross-cultural. Too often their interest stops at the borders of the nation-state where their research is centered, and they neither consider broader patterns nor make use of the comparative contrasts and differing methodological approaches offered by work on other parts of the region. While a common regional character can probably only be discerned from certain angles of observation, illuminating studies have resulted from such explorations.[7] It would also behoove Southeast Asianists to take a look at the concerns of other area studies, whose practitioners have often developed other disciplines and theoretical concerns. The currently fashionable field of postcolonialism has largely resulted from the introduction of an established South Asianist discourse into general academic consciousness; and I remember my own epiphany at discovering Africa, with its social anthropology and oral history, on joining London's School of Oriental and African Studies.

---

[7] For example, Oliver Wolters, *History, Culture and Region in Southeast Asian Perspective* (Singapore: Institute of Southeast Asian Studies, 1982), and Richard A. O'Connor, "'Agricultural Change and Ethnic

Hitherto, there has been a tacit assumption—by Americans, at least—that Southeast Asia has best been studied from the USA, that within the US various area programs and aspirant area programs compete for funds and prestige, and that each should aim for as broad an area and disciplinary coverage as possible in terms of both teaching and library resources. This is simply impractical nowadays. Moreover, it makes for parochialism, the wastage of resources, and a beggar-thy-neighbor attitude by individual scholars and centers. Unfortunately, it is difficult to avoid, given the fact that the current system of government support is based on competition between institutions. (Would it not offend many sensibilities, I would suggest it might be no bad thing if such subsidies were ended.)[8]

We need to emphasize cooperation rather than competition. We already have the Southeast Asia Summer Studies Institute, from whose success we can see the advantages to be had from drawing on a wide range of teaching resources and student exchange. Indeed, such a pooling of effort is a sheer necessity if we are to establish any real multidisciplinary balance. Earlier commentators on the state of Southeast Asia studies have pointed out the narrowness of the field's base in terms of language teaching and mastery. They have also noted the extreme skewing of research and teaching towards the

---

Succession in Southeast Asian States, A Case for Regional Anthropology," *Journal of Asian Studies* 54 (1995): 968–996.

[8] This is by no means the first time that the rigidities of the funding system have been criticized; see William H. Frederick, "Adapting the Area Study Center Concept to New Needs," in Ronald A. Morse, ed., *Southeast Asian Studies: Options for the Future* (Washington DC: Wilson Center East Asian Studies, 1984), pp. 87–94. Frederick made a number of proposals for rationalization and networking, unfortunately to little avail.

social sciences, which has played an important role in keeping Southeast Asia studies in the role of adjunct to disciplinary concerns rather than as an academic field of interest in itself.[9] New generations of students will only reinforce this imbalance unless we develop mechanisms whereby they have better access to training in Southeast Asian languages and humanities.

We need to think more in terms of networks than of institutions, and these networks should in principle be global and not just regional or national. The US may still have the advantage in academic training techniques and resources, but in Southeast Asia studies its lead today is marginal and diminishing. Patronage is no longer strongly tied to national interests, while foreign and international sources of project support are increasing.

Although one purpose of network-building would be to mobilize and rationalize the use of human and library resources within the field of Southeast Asia studies, there should also be a serious effort to develop networks extending beyond the regional specialists, in order to import experience and techniques from other areas and disciplines and to make Southeast Asianists' combination of local and disciplinary knowledge available to the wider scholarly world. This means, in the first place, identifying problems which are of broad concern intellectually and/or socially, to which the study of Southeast Asia can contribute significantly. (Bear in mind, this is not the same as using problem-orientation to avoid adequate grounding in local knowledge; rather, it requires building on such a foundation.) This can begin quite modestly, with greater efforts to reach out to other

---

[9] See the contributions to Charles Hirschman, Charles F. Keyes, and Karl Hutterer, eds., *Southeast Asian Studies in the Balance: Reflections from America* (Ann Arbor: Association for Asian Studies, 1992).

programs and disciplines within the university, especially the social sciences and humanities, for a greater exchange of knowledge and analytical techniques.

When I say this would be a modest beginning, I should stress that I mean financially rather than mentally, for such an apparently small change would involve very great alterations in our accustomed academic compartmentalization and competition, and our habit of rejecting as "peripheral" subjects which are not deeply and immediately involved in our own. This implies nothing less than the transformation of our universities, which in the last century have seen the rampant proliferation and specialization of disciplines. At present they rather resemble those colonies of sea creatures which, having established their individual compartments, extend themselves from it only far enough to capture such resources as may waft their way. The young may be mobile, but only until they too have created their niche. The whole may form an imposing structure, but it is hardly a flexible or efficient one, and the only thing it does really well is preserve the tranquillity of those within it. Attempts at integration through cross-disciplinary and cross-cultural programs have generally achieved at best a tolerated place on the academic periphery, and often they have not held that for long. Nonetheless it is clear that this mode of development has got out of hand, and academics in almost all fields are going to have to learn to organize themselves and their teaching in very different ways if they are to cope with the present proliferation and deconstruction of ways of understanding. The rethinking of area studies is therefore necessarily part of a larger task of academic reform.

Constructing networks beyond one's own university environment is not just a matter of the Internet and some more conferences. It needs to be collective and sustained, and it will involve changes in academic thinking which, if now increasingly discussed, are still far from being adopted. However, we can make a small beginning by improving the conditions for a sustained face-to-face exchange of ideas. We can try to make centers of Southeast Asia studies more user-friendly to outsiders, not only Southeast Asia specialists from other universities and countries but also non-Southeast Asia specialists who want to gain background relevant to their own fields of interest, whether that is philosophy or urban planning.

This last requires mental as well as mechanical adjustment. Too often Southeast Asianists—particularly those at the major centers of the area's study—draw a line between those who have language skills and broad area-focused training, who are therefore "really" knowledgeable, and those who may in fact have extensive on-the-ground experience in an area but know it from the angle of a particular specialization and do not wish to devote themselves primarily to the area's study. The latter are viewed as not really serious, as are students who wish to obtain knowledge of Southeast Asia but not for its own sake. However, the region's increased importance and ease of access means there are ever more such people, and the proliferation of relevant technical and economic expertise means that the "real" Southeast Asianists are likely to be a backwater rather than the forefront of knowledge in many respects. There needs to be greater humility and flexibility among the area experts, both in teaching and in mobilizing the expertise of non-Southeast Asianists with area experience.

We should try to develop modalities for extended exchanges of ideas, whether through simply encouraging people to spend time at a particular center of Southeast Asian studies for more than just a few conference or lecture days, arranging student and staff exchanges, or developing workshop series which, over a series of years, would consider different aspects of an important problem and which would center on but not be limited to Southeast Asian expertise and experience. "Masterclasses"—consisting of small groups of advanced graduate and post-doctoral students led by a prominent scholar and concentrating on a particular problem of study for, say, a week's intensive work—have recently been introduced by the International Institute of Asian Studies based in Leiden, and no doubt other innovative methods could be developed.[10] The important thing, though, is that such efforts seek to consolidate and not to proliferate bureaucratic structures, that they have a limited (if renewable) shelf-life, and that care is taken not to identify them with a single set of institutional interests.

Fundamental to any attempt to help Southeast Asianists break out of the area studies ghetto is the formulation of questions which cross disciplinary boundaries and whose investigation can serve to illuminate both theory and local knowledge. Once a number of these have been determined, we can consider how best they can be pursued in a sustained fashion. Craig Reynolds began this process in last year's Golay lecture, when he named several issues which needed comparative exploration in connection with

---

[10] This program, started in 1995, initially was centered on the research interests of Dutch graduate students, but it was intended to move as rapidly as possible to a European and then global level, this being thought essential both for significant recruitment and impact.

understanding changing Southeast Asian concepts of selfhood: literary production, religious reform movements, and disciplines of the body.

For my part, I might suggest that we take up topics which would help break down our shopworn but still powerful assumptions about the centrality of the nation-state, modernity, and western vs non-western, as an antidote to the country specialization which still dominates Southeast Asia studies. For example, we might investigate networks which go beyond the boundaries of state (and region). Until the end of the last century, at the least, Southeast Asian people's lives were dominated by religious, trading, and patronage relationships which had little to do with boundaries and hierarchy as defined by the state. For many, these have continued to have major importance. There are also new influences which bring the centrality of the nation-state into question—indeed, there is now even talk of the possibility of "virtual states" whose power is based on control of technology, knowledge, and investment rather than territory. In Southeast Asia we have been brought to a new awareness of transnational business and labor networks, ethnic diasporas, the influence of global corporations, and the creation of multinational entities such as ASEAN and "growth triangles." I would hope that we can look at such flows of ideas, power, and population, past as well as present, making use of the comparative knowledge and theoretical expertise of scholars from different disciplines and regional backgrounds.

I would also hope to see studies which would break down the artificial boundaries between "traditional" and "modern." It is of course no longer fashionable to talk of societies as "traditional," but one way or another the traditional-modern contrast remains firmly ingrained in our minds. We study things that are in the past, or on the periphery, in contrast to where we are (which we assume to be up-to-date, at the center). We need to be more fluid in our understanding of civilizations, of the way in which the past lives in the present and beyond it, of how certain issues, such as the getting of power and the shaping of ideas, are related to the cultural, economic, and technological environment in which they appear. Modernity is certainly not a steady state, and our notion of what is modern will not be how our descendants conceive it. And there is no reason at all to think that modernity will be continue to be formulated in the west.

The "western-nonwestern" contrast is another persistent boundary that I would like to see dissolved. I must confess that I have particular trouble with it because I live in a country that I find familiar from previous experience living in rural Thailand, and not at all from living in England, the Netherlands, or the United States. Yet few would call Italy non-western, and if you do it raises the question of where the west lies and what the content of western civilization is. In point of fact, our ideas of "western" are based on an idealized notion of North Atlantic values and experience, and we tend to ignore or push aside as marginal all the many things which don't fit.

Culture and civilization must be considered much more subtly and flexibly, especially by social scientists; and in particular the assumed connection between culture and modernity must be dissolved. Here the development of "cultural studies" as a way of blurring the boundary between the social sciences and humanities is particularly important. Incorporating some of this approach should be particularly fruitful for Southeast Asian studies, where "literature" has generally been viewed by other disciplines as, at best, something that can be employed to illustrate changing social and political attitudes.

It is also important, I think, to consider more deeply the ways in which the peoples of Southeast Asia accumulate and organize knowledge. Comparative attention has been given to state efforts at employing schooling to shape people's attitudes towards hierarchy and legitimacy,[11] but we also need to explore the older sources and understandings of knowledge, and the way in which these continue to affect the content and organization of thought. And we need to consider in a more systematic way the effect of mass media and globalization on the shaping of knowledge.[12]

I'd also like to see a broader consideration of the process—cultural as well as socio-economic and ecological—of Southeast Asia's industrialization. The recently fashionable field of "postcolonial studies" approaches such transformation in what seems to me an old-fashioned and negative way, emphasizing as it does cultural loss and portraying non-western modernity as a parody of the west.[13] Of course, western (and

---

[11] Charles F. Keyes, ed., *Reshaping Local Worlds: Formal Education and Cultural Change in Southeast Asia* (New Haven: Yale University Southeast Asian Studies, 1991).

[12] Benedict Anderson's *Imagined Communities* (London: Verso, rev. ed. 1991) traced the way in which print capitalism gave birth to the idea of the nation; it seems likely that the new media, with their even broader social and geographical reach, will also have a profound impact on the way in which the people of Southeast Asia see the world.

[13] A succinct but eloquent protest against this assumption is made in Janadas Devan's letter on "The Singapore Way," published in *The New York Review of Books*, June 6, 1996, pp. 65–66. A sigificant effort towards an interdisciplinary understanding of capitalist Southeast

particularly US) styles have recently had powerful influence on Southeast Asian tastes, just as French did in eighteenth-century Europe, but we mustn't confuse fashion with the more fundamental processes of economic and cultural change. We are *all* caught up in a process of transformation which can neither be rejected (for long) nor reversed, and we don't know where it is leading. It affects everybody; we are all in the process of becoming something other than what we were. Southeast Asia, with its diversity of cultures and economies, and its current rapid transformation, is an excellent vantage point from which to see the delineation of this new world.

In considering the impact of industrialization, we should not lose sight of its effect on Southeast Asia's rural areas. Rural-urban ties, or the lack of them, become crucial culturally, economically, and politically as rapid shifts in economic power and values destroy old ideas of legitimacy and patterns of deference. New sources of leadership arise in the countryside and towns, which may align the populace with urban authority and values, may hold forth an alternative way of life, or may simply exploit those under their thumb. In Southeast Asia's current flux, there is a great blurring of the lines between crime and legality, legitimacy and illegitimacy, predation and governance, and this is most vividly experienced in the areas on the fault line between rural and urban cultures. We must try to discern how people experience these confusions, and with what ideas they seek to defend themselves.

A multidisciplinary investigation of environmental issues would be an especially fruitful way of looking at

---

Asian society is being undertaken in Australia by Murdoch University's ambitious project on the "new rich" in Asia.

this changing world, not only because Southeast Asia has wide-ranging natural resources and a currently rapid rate of degradation, but because it could bring together the natural sciences as well as the social sciences and humanities. The barrier between the "hard" and "soft" sciences, the study of the world and the study of man, is dissolving with our increasing recognition that all rules are propositions and that universal properties are affected by time. We must realize that it is an illusion to aim for the social sciences to acquire the "certainties" of natural sciences, and recognize rather that these fields of knowledge exist in relation to each other, and can fulfill each other.

Finally, I would hope that the variety of Southeast Asia's civilization, its possession of notable ancient and modern high cultures, can lead its specialists to take an active role in promoting cultural studies which would go beyond the national boundaries at which most now stop, and consider the relationship between cultures, the way in which cultural influences flow from one part of the world to another and are re-imagined there.

Of course, this is just one person's wish list. We need to have the input of many other scholars, and not just Southeast Asianists, if we are going to formulate a balanced agenda for integrating studies of the region with theoretical and practical questions of fundamental importance. This will need to be a broad collective effort, involving global input, but we must start somewhere. One beginning that could be made with Cornell's resources is to devote future lectures in this series to opening up discussions along such lines. This would be very much in Frank Golay's inquiring and interdisciplinary spirit, and his concern that Southeast Asia be seen in its global context. Lauriston Sharp once remarked that Frank Golay rescued the Southeast Asia

Program at several times of crisis in its early development; perhaps his spirit can perform the same service in its later age.

# FRANK HINDMAN GOLAY, 1915–1990

## Biography

Frank Hindman Golay came to Cornell University in 1953 as an assistant professor of economics and Asian studies. He became a full professor in 1962, chaired the Department of Economics in the mid-sixties, and directed the university's Southeast Asia Program from 1970 to 1976. In the long span of his active career as an economist and scholar of economic history in the Philippines, he also served as director for the Southeast Asia Program's Philippine Project, director of the London-Cornell Project on Southeast Asia, chairman of the Philippines Council of the Asia Foundation, and president of the Association for Asian Studies. For his scholarship on the Philippines, Professor Golay was awarded an honorary L.L.D. degree by the Ateneo de Manila in 1966, and he received fellowships from the Guggenheim and Luce foundations, the Social Science Research Council, the National Endowment for the Humanities, and the United States Educational Foundation (Fulbright).

When Frank Golay arrived at Cornell, the Southeast Asia Program was newly established. With steady good judgment, Professor Golay helped to foster and direct the young, interdisciplinary program and its growing collection of library research materials. According to Professor Lauriston Sharp, it was Frank Golay who "at least twice during the zigzag history of the program, prevented its foundering and set it again on its way." Thoughout those same years, Professor Golay pursued his research into the Philippines, research that earned him his high reputation as a meticulously thorough, innovative scholar. Professor Golay's bibliography is included here. His example and his work continue to inspire us.

## Introduction to Bibliography

In 1993, with great fanfare, the World Bank published a report entitled *The East Asian Miracle: Economic Growth and Public Policy*. The report argued that interventionist economic policies implemented by strong bureaucratic institutions had complemented market-oriented strategies in eight "high-performing Asian economies." To many American scholars of Northeast Asia, this point was already orthodoxy; political scientists in particular had for some time made the case for *dirigisme* over free markets to explain the rapid pace of economic growth in that region. The World Bank report also considered the experiences of four Southeast Asian nations. Again, its conclusions corresponded with those of a number of area specialists. For by the late 1980s a group of "new institutionalists" had begun to examine the role of a disciplined, activist state in the promotion of economic growth in Southeast Asia. Their approach to political economy helped to initiate one of the most innovative fields of Southeast Asia scholarship in the 1990s.

The work of Frank H. Golay anticipated this entire line of analysis. Three full decades before the appearance of the World Bank's report and the rise of new institutional political economy in Southeast Asian studies, Professor Golay began to devote scholarly energy, sympathy, and insight to an examination of the relationship between state policy and economic growth in Southeast Asia. Reaching far beyond the increasingly narrow confines of economics, the discipline in which he was trained, he took firm hold of historical and institutional data in fashioning his analyses. Professor Golay's 1976 article on "Southeast Asia: the 'Colonial Drain' Revisited" and his contributions to the 1969 volume, *Underdevelopment and Economic Nationalism in Southeast Asia*, set a high and still pertinent standard in using those data to inform contemporary political economy. Balance, too, distinguishes Professor Golay's writings. His prescient *The Philippines: Public Policy and National Economic Development* takes as its premise the assertion that the old controversy of "state vs. market" deserves research and thought rather than politicization.

Professor Golay devoted the bulk of his career to the study of the Philippines. The authors of *The East Asian Miracle* never included that nation among the "high performing Asian economies" examined in their study. The events of the 1980s had excluded it from that group, for reasons addressed in detail and with his customary balance in Professor Golay's 1986 presidential address to the Association for Asian Studies. Still, sampling Professor Golay's writings on the Philippines—including, no doubt, his forthcoming book on the American colonial period, to be posthumously published—can only profit readers who seek to understand the unprecedented economic change which has come to Southeast Asia in the last decade.

# FRANK H. GOLAY
# BIBLIOGRAPHY

*Pattern of Imperialism: Philippine-American Relations* (tentative title). Madison, Wisconsin: Center for Southeast Asian Studies, 1996.

"AAS Presidential Address: Cause for Concern in the Philippines,' *Journal of Asian Studies*, XLV, 5 (November 1986): pp. 935-943.

"Manila Americans and Philippine Policy: The Voice of American Business" and 'Taming the American Multinationals." In *The Philippine Economy and the United States*, edited by Norman G. Owen. Michigan Papers on South and Southeast Asia, no. 22 (1984).

"Social and Economic Problems Facing the Philippines, 1983-2000." Background paper, Canadian International Development Agency (August 1983): 1-19.

Golay, Frank H., Guy J. Pauker and Cynthia H. Enloe. *Diversity and Development in Southeast Asia*. New York: McGraw-Hill, 1977.

"Some Unintended Consequences of Mutual Free Trade." *Bulletin of the American Historical Collection*, 4 (October 1977): 46-57.

"The 'Colonial Drain' Revisited." In *Southeast Asian History and Historiography*, edited by C.D. Cowan and O.W. Wolters. Essays presented to D.G.E. Hall. Ithaca: Cornell University Press, 1976.

"The Philippine-U.S. Relationship: Trade." In *The Philippine–American Relationship*, edited by James Hoyt. Manila: USIS, 1976.

"Philippine Economic Nationalism: The Drive to Indigenize." *Solidarity*, 7 (February 1972): 2-20.

"Some Costs of Philippine Politics." *Asia* (Autumn 1971): 45-61.

Golay, Frank H., Thomas McHale and George Taylor. "Background Paper." In *U.S.–Philippine Economic Relations*. Special Report Series, no. 12. Washington, DC: Center for Strategic and International Studies, 1971.

Golay, Frank H., Ralph Anspach, M. Ruth Pfanner and Eliezer B. Ayal. *Underdevelopment and Economic Nationalism in Southeast Asia*, edited by Frank H. Golay. Ithaca: Cornell University Press, 1969.

"The Philippine Economy." In *Six Perspectives on the Philippines*, edited by George M. Guthrie. Manila: Bookmark, 1968.

"Philippine-American Affairs in 1966 and 1967." *Solidarity*, 3 (October 1968): 20-37.

Golay, Frank H. and Marvin E. Goodstein. *Philippine Rice Needs in 1990, Output and Input Requirements*. Manila: Agency for International Development, 1967.

*The United States and the Philippines*. New York: Prentice-Hall, 1966.

"Philippine-American Affairs: The Case for Disengagement." *Asia*, 6 (Autumn 1966): 73-92.

"Obstacles to Philippine Economic Planning." *The Philippine Economic Journal*, 4, second semester (1965): 284-309.

Hartendorp, A.V.H. *The Santo Tomas Story*, edited by Frank H. Golay. New York: McGraw-Hill, 1964.

*The Philippines: Public Policy and National Economic Development*. Ithaca: Cornell University Press, 1961.

"Entrepreneurship and Economic Development in the Philippines." *Far Eastern Survey*, 29 (June 1960): 81-87.

"The Quirino Administration in Perspective." *Far Eastern Survey*, 28 (March 1969): 40-45.

"Commercial Policy and Economic Nationalism." *Quarterly Journal of Economics*, 72 (November 1958): 574-587.

*The Revised US–Philippine Trade Agreement of 1955*, Cornell Southeast Asia Program Data Paper, 23 (November 1956).

"The Emerging Alternative to Develuation." *Philippine Studies*, 4 (September 1956): 373-389.

"The Philippine Monetary Policy Debate." *Pacific Affairs*, 29 (September 1956): 253-264.

"The Case for Peso Devaluation." *Philippine Law Journal*, 31 (September 1956): 498-519.

"Another Look at the Revised Philippine-US Trade Agreement." *Economic Research Journal*, 3 (June 1956): 18-27.

"Economic Aspects of Philippine Agrarian Reform." *Philippine Sociological Review*, IV (January 1956): 20-32.

"Economic Consequences of the US–Philippine Trade Agreement." *Pacific Affairs*, 28 (March 1955): 53-70.

"Economic Problems Facing Post-Treaty Japan." *Federal Reserve Bulletin*, 38 (January 1952): 11-21.

"The International Wheat Agreement." *Quarterly Journal of Economics*, 64 (August 1950): 442-463.

## SOUTHEAST ASIA PROGRAM PUBLICATIONS
### Cornell University

#### Studies on Southeast Asia

Number 24   *Paths to Conflagration: Fifty Years of Diplomacy and Warfare in Laos, Thailand, and Vietnam, 1778-1828,* Mayoury Ngaosyvathn and Pheuiphanh Ngaosyvathn. 1998. 268 pp. ISBN 0-87727-723-0.

Number 23   *Nguyễn Cochinchina: Southern Vietnam in the Seventeenth and Eighteenth Centuries,* Li Tana. 1998. 194 pp. ISBN 0-87727-722-2.

Number 22   *Young Heroes: The Indonesian Family in Politics,* Saya S. Shiraishi. 1997. 183 pp. ISBN 0-87727-721-4

Number 21   *Interpreting Development: Capitalism, Democracy, and the Middle Class in Thailand,* John Girling. 1996. 95 pp. ISBN 0-87727-720-6

Number 20   *Making Indonesia,* ed. Daniel S. Lev, Ruth McVey. 1996. 201 pp. ISBN 0-87727-719-2

Number 19   *Essays into Vietnamese Pasts,* ed. K. W. Taylor, John K. Whitmore. 1995. 288 pp. ISBN 0-87727-718-4

Number 18   *In the Land of Lady White Blood: Southern Thailand and the Meaning of History,* Lorraine M. Gesick. 1995. 106 pp. ISBN 0-87727-717-6

Number 17   *The Vernacular Press and the Emergence of Modern Indonesian Consciousness,* Ahmat Adam. 1995. 220 pp. ISBN 0-87727-716-8

Number 16   *The Nan Chronicle,* trans., ed. David K. Wyatt. 1994. 158 pp. ISBN 0-87727-715-X

Number 15   *Selective Judicial Competence: The Cirebon-Priangan Legal Administration, 1680–1792,* Mason C. Hoadley. 1994. 185 pp. ISBN 0-87727-714-1

Number 14   *Sjahrir: Politics and Exile in Indonesia,* Rudolf Mrázek. 1994. 536 pp. ISBN 0-87727-713-3

| | |
|---|---|
| Number 13 | *Fair Land Sarawak: Some Recollections of an Expatriate Officer*, Alastair Morrison. 1993. 196 pp. ISBN 0-87727-712-5 |
| Number 12 | *Fields from the Sea: Chinese Junk Trade with Siam during the Late Eighteenth and Early Nineteenth Centuries*, Jennifer Cushman. 1993. 206 pp. ISBN 0-87727-711-7 |
| Number 11 | *Money, Markets, and Trade in Early Southeast Asia: The Development of Indigenous Monetary Systems to AD 1400*, Robert S. Wicks. 1992. 2nd printing 1996. 354 pp., 78 tables, illus., maps. ISBN 0-87727-710-9 |
| Number 10 | *Tai Ahoms and the Stars: Three Ritual Texts to Ward Off Danger*, trans., ed. B. J. Terwiel, Ranoo Wichasin. 1992. 170 pp. ISBN 0-87727-709-5 |
| Number 9 | *Southeast Asian Capitalists*, ed. Ruth McVey. 1992. 2nd printing 1993. 220 pp. ISBN 0-87727-708-7 |
| Number 8 | *The Politics of Colonial Exploitation: Java, the Dutch, and the Cultivation System*, Cornelis Fasseur, ed. R. E. Elson, trans. R. E. Elson, Ary Kraal. 1992. 2nd printing 1994. 266 pp. ISBN 0-87727-707-9 |
| Number 7 | *A Malay Frontier: Unity and Duality in a Sumatran Kingdom*, Jane Drakard. 1990. 215 pp. ISBN 0-87727-706-0 |
| Number 6 | *Trends in Khmer Art*, Jean Boisselier, ed. Natasha Eilenberg, trans. Natasha Eilenberg, Melvin Elliott. 1989. 124 pp., 24 plates. ISBN 0-87727-705-2 |
| Number 5 | *Southeast Asian Ephemeris: Solar and Planetary Positions, A.D. 638–2000*, J. C. Eade. 1989. 175 pp. ISBN 0-87727-704-4 |
| Number 3 | *Thai Radical Discourse: The Real Face of Thai Feudalism Today*, Craig J. Reynolds. 1987. 2nd printing 1994. 186 pp. ISBN 0-87727-702-8 |
| Number 1 | *The Symbolism of the Stupa*, Adrian Snodgrass. 1985. Revised with index, 1988. 2nd printing 1991. 469 pp. ISBN 0-87727-700-1 |

## SEAP Series

| | |
|---|---|
| Number 16 | *Cutting Across the Lands: An Annotated Bibliography on Natural Resource Management and Community Development in Indonesia, the Philippines, and Malaysia*, ed. Eveline Ferretti. 1997. 329 pp. ISBN 0-87727-133-X |
| Number 15 | *The Revolution Falters: The Left in Philippine Politics After 1986*, ed. Patricio N. Abinales. 1996. 182 pp. ISBN 0-87727-132-1 |
| Number 14 | *Being Kammu: My Village, My Life*, ed. Damrong Tayanin. 1994. 138 pp., 22 tables, illus., maps. ISBN 0-87727-130-5 |
| Number 13 | *The American War in Vietnam*, ed. Jayne Werner, David Hunt. 1993. 132 pp. ISBN 0-87727-131-3 |
| Number 12 | *The Voice of Young Burma*, Aye Kyaw. 1993. 98 pp. ISBN 0-87727-129-1 |
| Number 11 | *The Political Legacy of Aung San*, ed. Josef Silverstein. Revised edition 1993. 169 pp. ISBN 0-87727-128-3 |
| Number 10 | *Studies on Vietnamese Language and Literature: A Preliminary Bibliography*, Nguyen Dinh Tham. 1992. 227 pp. ISBN 0-87727-127-5 |
| Number 9 | *A Secret Past*, Dokmaisot, trans. Ted Strehlow. 1992. 2nd printing 1997. 72 pp. ISBN 0-87727-126-7 |
| Number 8 | *From PKI to the Comintern, 1924–1941: The Apprenticeship of the Malayan Communist Party*, Cheah Boon Kheng. 1992. 147 pp. ISBN 0-87727-125-9 |
| Number 7 | *Intellectual Property and US Relations with Indonesia, Malaysia, Singapore, and Thailand*, Elisabeth Uphoff. 1991. 67 pp. ISBN 0-87727-124-0 |
| Number 6 | *The Rise and Fall of the Communist Party of Burma (CPB)*, Bertil Lintner. 1990. 124 pp. 26 illus., 14 maps. ISBN 0-87727-123-2 |

Number 5    *Japanese Relations with Vietnam: 1951–1987,*
            Masaya Shiraishi. 1990. 174 pp.
            ISBN 0-87727-122-4

Number 3    *Postwar Vietnam: Dilemmas in Socialist
            Development,* ed. Christine White, David Marr.
            1988. 2nd printing 1993. 260 pp.
            ISBN 0-87727-120-8

Number 2    *The Dobama Movement in Burma (1930–1938),*
            Khin Yi. 1988. 160 pp. ISBN 0-87727-118-6

## Translation Series

Volume 4    *Approaching Suharto's Indonesia from the Margins,*
            ed. Takashi Shiraishi. 1994. 153 pp.
            ISBN 0-87727-403-7

Volume 3    *The Japanese in Colonial Southeast Asia,* ed. Saya
            Shiraishi, Takashi Shiraishi. 1993. 172 pp.
            ISBN 0-87727-402-9

Volume 2    *Indochina in the 1940s and 1950s,* ed. Takashi
            Shiraishi, Motoo Furuta. 1992. 196 pp.
            ISBN 0-87727-401-0

Volume 1    *Reading Southeast Asia,* ed. Takashi Shiraishi.
            1990. 188 pp. ISBN 0-87727-400-2


## CORNELL MODERN INDONESIA PROJECT PUBLICATIONS

### Cornell University

Number 74   *The Roots of Acehnese Rebellion 1989–1992,* Tim
            Kell. 1995. 103 pp. ISBN 0-87763-040-2

Number 73   *"White Book" on the 1992 General Election in
            Indonesia,* trans. Dwight King. 1994. 72 pp.
            ISBN 0-87763-039-9

Number 72   *Popular Indonesian Literature of the Qur'an,*
            Howard M. Federspiel. 1994. 170 pp.
            ISBN 0-87763-038-0

Number 71  *A Javanese Memoir of Sumatra, 1945–1946: Love and Hatred in the Liberation War*, Takao Fusayama. 1993. 150 pp. ISBN 0-87763-037-2

Number 70  *East Kalimantan: The Decline of a Commercial Aristocracy*, Burhan Magenda. 1991. 120 pp. ISBN 0-87763-036-4

Number 69  *The Road to Madiun: The Indonesian Communist Uprising of 1948*, Elizabeth Ann Swift. 1989. 120 pp. ISBN 0-87763-035-6

Number 68  *Intellectuals and Nationalism in Indonesia: A Study of the Following Recruited by Sutan Sjahrir in Occupation Jakarta*, J. D. Legge. 1988. 159 pp. ISBN 0-87763-034-8

Number 67  *Indonesia Free: A Biography of Mohammad Hatta*, Mavis Rose. 1987. 252 pp. ISBN 0-87763-033-X

Number 66  *Prisoners at Kota Cane*, Leon Salim, trans. Audrey Kahin. 1986. 112 pp. ISBN 0-87763-032-1

Number 65  *The Kenpeitai in Java and Sumatra*, trans. Barbara G. Shimer, Guy Hobbs, intro. Theodore Friend. 1986. 80 pp. ISBN 0-87763-031-3

Number 64  *Suharto and His Generals: Indonesia's Military Politics, 1975–1983*, David Jenkins. 1984. 4th printing 1997. 300 pp. ISBN 0-87763-030-5

Number 62  *Interpreting Indonesian Politics: Thirteen Contributions to the Debate, 1964–1981*, ed. Benedict Anderson, Audrey Kahin, intro. Daniel S. Lev. 1982. 3rd printing 1991. 172 pp. ISBN 0-87763-028-3

Number 61  *Sickle and Crescent: The Communist Revolt of 1926 in Banten*, Michael C. Williams. 1982. 81 pp. ISBN 0-87763-027-5

Number 60  *The Minangkabau Response to Dutch Colonial Rule in the Nineteenth Century*, Elizabeth E. Graves. 1981. 157 pp. ISBN 0-87763-000-3

Number 59  *Breaking the Chains of Oppression of the Indonesian People: Defense Statement at His Trial on Charges of Insulting the Head of State, Bandung, June 7–10, 1979,* Heri Akhmadi. 1981. 201 pp. ISBN 0-87763-001-1

Number 58  *Administration of Islam in Indonesia,* Deliar Noer. 1978. 82 pp. ISBN 0-87763-002-X

Number 57  *Permesta: Half a Rebellion,* Barbara S. Harvey. 1977. 174 pp. ISBN 0-87763-003-8

Number 55  *Report from Banaran: The Story of the Experiences of a Soldier during the War of Independence,* Maj. Gen. T. B. Simatupang. 1972. 186 pp. ISBN 0-87763-005-4

Number 52  *A Preliminary Analysis of the October 1 1965, Coup in Indonesia (Prepared in January 1966),* Benedict R. Anderson, Ruth T. McVey, assist. Frederick P. Bunnell. 1971. 3rd printing 1990. 174 pp. ISBN 0-87763-008-9

Number 51  *The Putera Reports: Problems in Indonesian-Japanese War-Time Cooperation,* Mohammad Hatta, trans., intro. William H. Frederick. 1971. 114 pp. ISBN 0-87763-009-7

Number 50  *Schools and Politics: The Kaum Muda Movement in West Sumatra (1927–1933),* Taufik Abdullah. 1971. 257 pp. ISBN 0-87763-010-0

Number 49  *The Foundation of the Partai Muslimin Indonesia,* K. E. Ward. 1970. 75 pp. ISBN 0-87763-011-9

Number 48  *Nationalism, Islam and Marxism,* Soekarno, intro. Ruth T. McVey. 1970. 2nd printing 1984. 62 pp. ISBN 0-87763-012-7

Number 43  *State and Statecraft in Old Java: A Study of the Later Mataram Period, 16th to 19th Century,* Soemarsaid Moertono. Revised edition 1981. 180 pp. ISBN 0-87763-017-8

Number 37  *Mythology and the Tolerance of the Javanese,* Benedict R. O'G. Anderson. 2nd edition 1997. 104 pp., 65 illus. ISBN 0-87763-041-0

Number  25  *The Communist Uprisings of 1926–1927 in Indonesia: Key Documents*, ed., intro. Harry J. Benda, Ruth T. McVey. 1960. 2nd printing 1969. 177 pp. ISBN 0-87763-024-0

Number  7  *The Soviet View of the Indonesian Revolution*, Ruth T. McVey. 1957. 3rd printing 1969. 90 pp. ISBN 0-87763-018-6

Number  6  *The Indonesian Elections of 1955*, Herbert Feith. 1957. 2nd printing 1971. 91 pp. ISBN 0-87763-020-8

## LANGUAGE TEXTS

INDONESIAN

*Beginning Indonesian Through Self-Instruction,* John U. Wolff, Dédé Oetomo, Daniel Fietkiewicz. 3rd revised edition 1992. 3 volume set. 1,057 pp. ISBN 0-87727-519-X

*Indonesian Readings,* John U. Wolff. 1978. 4th printing 1992. 480 pp. ISBN 0-87727-517-3

*Indonesian Conversations,* John U. Wolff. 1978. 3rd printing 1991. 297 pp. ISBN 0-87727-516-5

*Formal Indonesian,* John U. Wolff. 2nd revised edition 1986. 446 pp. ISBN 0-87727-515-7

TAGALOG

*Pilipino Through Self-Instruction,* John U. Wolff, Ma. Theresa C. Centano, Der-Hwa U. Rau. 1991. 4 volume set. 1,490 pp. ISBN 0-87727-524-6

THAI

*A. U. A. Language Center Thai Course Book 1,* J. Marvin Brown. Originally published by the American University Alumni Association Language Center, 1974. Reissued by Cornell Southeast Asia Program,1991. 267 pp. ISBN 0-87727-506-8

*A. U. A. Language Center Thai Course Book 2,* 1992. 288 pp. ISBN 0-87727-507-6

*A. U. A. Language Center Thai Course Book 3,* 1992. 247 pp. ISBN 0-87727-508-4

*A. U. A. Language Center Thai Course, Reading and Writing Text (mostly reading),* 1979. Reissued 1997. 164 pp. ISBN 0-87727-511-4

*A. U. A. Language Center Thai Course, Reading and Writing Workbook (mostly writing),* 1979. Reissued 1997. 99 pp. ISBN 0-87727-512-2

KHMER

*Cambodian System of Writing and Beginning Reader,* Franklin E. Huffman. Originally published by Yale University Press, 1970. Reissued by Cornell Southeast Asia Program, 3rd printing 1992. 365 pp. ISBN 0-300-01314-0

*Modern Spoken Cambodian,* Franklin E. Huffman, assist. Charan Promchan, Chhom-Rak Thong Lambert. Originally published by Yale University Press, 1970. Reissued by Cornell Southeast Asia Program, 3rd printing 1991. 451 pp. ISBN 0-300-01316-7

*Intermediate Cambodian Reader,* ed. Franklin E. Huffman, assist. Im Proum. Originally published by Yale University Press, 1972. Reissued by Cornell Southeast Asia Program, 1988. 499 pp. ISBN 0-300-01552-6

*Cambodian Literary Reader and Glossary,* Franklin E. Huffman, Im Proum. Originally published by Yale University Press, 1977. Reissued by Cornell Southeast Asia Program, 1988. 494 pp. ISBN 0-300-02069-4

HMONG

*White Hmong-English Dictionary,* Ernest E. Heimbach. 1969. 7th printing 1997. 523 pp. ISBN 0-87727-075-9

VIETNAMESE

*Intermediate Spoken Vietnamese,* Franklin E. Huffman, Tran Trong Hai. 1980. 3rd printing 1994. ISBN 0-87727-500-9

\* \* \*

*Southeast Asian Studies: Reorientations.* Craig J. Reynolds and Ruth McVey. Frank H. Golay Lectures 2 & 3. 70 pp. ISBN 0-87727-301-4

*Javanese Literature in Surakarta Manuscripts,* Nancy K. Florida. Hard cover series ISBN 0-87727-600-5; Paperback series ISBN 0-87727-601-3. Vol. 1, *Introduction and Manuscripts of the Karaton Surakarta.* 1993. 410 pp. Frontispiece, 5 illus. Hard cover, ISBN 0-87727-602-1, Paperback, ISBN 0-87727-603-X

*Sbek Thom: Khmer Shadow Theater.* Pech Tum Kravel, trans. Sos Kem, ed. Thavro Phim, Sos Kem, Martin Hatch. 1996. 363 pp., 153 photographs. ISBN 0-87727-620-X

*In the Mirror, Literature and Politics in Siam in the American Era,* ed. Benedict R. O'G. Anderson, trans. Benedict R. O'G. Anderson, Ruchira Mendiones. 1985. 2nd printing 1991. 303 pp. Paperback. ISBN 974-210-380-1

To order*, please contact:

Cornell University
SEAP Distribution Center
369 Pine Tree Rd.
Ithaca, NY 14850-2819 USA

Tel: (607) 255-8038
Fax: (607) 255-7534

E-mail: SEAP-Pubs@cornell.edu
Web page (credit card orders): www.einaudi/cornell.edu
/SoutheastAsia/SEAPubs.html

* Orders must be prepaid by check or credit card.

www.ingramcontent.com/pod-product-compliance
Lightning Source LLC
Chambersburg PA
CBHW070310230426
43664CB00015B/2711